THE MIXER'S MANUAL

THE COCKTAIL BIBLE FOR SERIOUS DRINKERS | DAN JONES

THE MIXER'S MANUAL

THE COCKTAIL BIBLE FOR SERIOUS DRINKERS | DAN JONES

hardie grant books
MELBOURNE · LONDON

CONTENTS

THE DEPARTMENT OF RECREATIONAL DRINKING TECHNICAL GUIDE

INTRODUCTION

This is **The Mixer's Manual**. How to mix it, shake it, stir it and drink it: the all-in-one to get things done. A full cocktail list of classic recipes, tropical wonders and tiki power-punches; contemporary concoctions, emergency 3 a.m. store cupboard solutions, bacon infusions and the perfect Bloody Mary (page 82). Plus, homemade syrups and sours, retro greatest hits and eye-popping ideas with pickle juice. A perfectly mixed cocktail truly takes the edge off, underlining the mood, smoothing things out or peps them up again. A Brandy Alexander (page 117) should slip down like no-one's business, whereas a Wasabian (page 85) – fired up with wasabi – takes a bit of derring-do. Thirsty to master home mixology? This is the manual to show you how to do it.

Part One:
THE SET UP

1

THE TOOL BOX

Dry ice, distillation kits, masticating juicers: some take the maximalist approach to gadgetry. They're also the people who have a bread machine in a cupboard, collecting dust, or a toasted sandwich maker, crusted with cheese. Don't let your home bar look like a cocktail graveyard. Start off simple: a shaker, a bar spoon, a Hawthorne strainer, an ice bucket. Here's what you'll need to keep it minimal…

⊙ THE SHAKER

The mixer's silver bullet, the shaker is your single most important piece of kit – very few cocktails are possible without one. The classic metallic model has three main parts: a base, known as the 'can' (a tall, tumbler shape that tapers out), a tight-fitting funnel top with built-in strainer, onto which a small cap fits (which can also be used as a jigger). It's brilliantly straightforward, and like all the finest tools, it pays to keep it scrupulously clean.

If you don't have a shaker: consider the pickle jar with lid – sterilised, washed and rinsed – which can be an excellent stand-in when you're between shakers.

⊘ THE MIXING GLASS

A simple, sturdy straight-sided glass (also known as the Boston) for cocktails that need stirring with a bar spoon rather than shaking, or allows for extra volume when attached to the can of your shaker (the two halves are locked together, and the home mixer can shake until the drink is chilled). Then a Hawthorne strainer can be used to strain the drink into a glass.

If you don't have a mixing glass: use a straight-sided pint glass that tapers out and will fit into the can of your shaker, should you need it to.

⊙ THE JIGGER

Another essential for the toolbox. The standard measure for spirits and liqueurs, and available in many different sizes. Heavy, metallic jiggers look the part, but plastic or glass versions also do the job.

If you don't have a jigger: you should cross your fingers and free-pour your drinks. Or use an egg cup – at least then your ratios will be right, even if your shots might be a little over-generous.

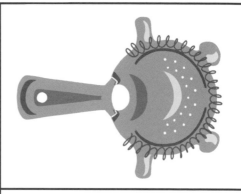

⊙ THE HAWTHORN STRAINER

The showy-looking strainer, seemingly trimmed with a spring, that comes in handy when your shaker's built-in version isn't up to the job. Place on a glass and pour the cocktail through it, or hold up against the cocktail can or mixing glass and pour from a height. Wash immediately after use.

If you don't have a Hawthorne strainer: use a tea strainer. It works brilliantly, but a Hawthorne really looks the part.

THE MINI SIEVE ⊙

Perfect for straining tiny pieces of ice, lemon pips, and other surprises from your drinks. Not essential, but great to have to hand.

If you don't have a mini sieve: use a large one. It can be messy, and sometimes a little floury, but it does the job when an emergency cocktail is required.

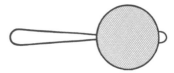

⊕ THE BLENDER

Essential for fruity numbers – but most domestic blenders find ice a little difficult, so it's best to use crushed ice in blender cocktails, rather than cubes or rocks. Add your ingredients first, then the ice and start off on a slow speed before turning it up to max. No need to strain, once the consistency is super-smooth, pour into a glass and serve.

If you don't have a blender: try a hand-held blender – again, only use crushed ice. Best for single cocktails.

⊕ THE CANELE KNIFE

A fancy bit of kit: the canele knife has a V-shaped groove for cutting citrus peel spirals, carving melons and probably many other crafty uses.

If you don't have a canele knife, use a small paring knife.

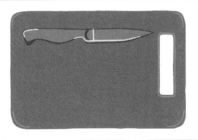

⊕ THE CHOPPING BOARD AND KNIFE

Simple, but essential. Keep the board clean, the knife super sharp.

THE ICE RING ➲

An ice ring is a fancy edition to a punch bowl – thawing slowly and adding subtle flavour to proceedings. It's easy to make and, packed with citrus slices, berries and herbs, certainly looks the part. Line a large plastic bowl with the appropriate garnishes, add add a smaller, weighty bowl. Add a bag or two of frozen peas to the smaller bowl, weighing it down so the water freezes into a ring. Fill the larger bowl from ⅓ to ½ full with filtered water, and freeze.

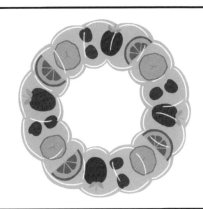

⤒ THE ICE BUCKET

The centrepiece of your home bar; simple, functional and slightly retro, or the full plastic pineapple. An insulated ice bucket means your ice cubes will keep their shape for longer, and a good set of tongs adds a touch of class.

If you don't have an ice bucket: use a glass bowl, a bowler hat, half a football, or a real metal bucket.

⤒ THE CHEESE CLOTH

For the specialist mixer, but essential when making infusions or using oils or fats to flavour alcohol. Use it clean and dispose after use.

If you don't have cheese cloth: use any clean, fine gauge material you don't mind throwing away afterwards. But try sticking to cheese cloth.

⊕ THE ICE PICK

Buy bags of crushed ice or cubes (and always buy double or triple the amount you think you'll need), or pummel your own homemade ice block with an ice pick. Boil water, let it cool slightly and pour into an old plastic ice-cream container. Freeze solid, turn out onto a clean tea towel, and then attack as needed with a firm grip. The ice will go everywhere, but bear with it. Keep the rocks large and jagged for drinks like Old Fashioned (page 41).

If you don't have an ice pick, don't use a knife as a substitute. Just learn from your mistakes and acquire one as soon as you can.

⊕ THE MUDDLER

A short, usually wooden baton used to mash and muddle fruit, herbs, ice and sugar in the glass, bruising and bashing up your ingredients to release their natural oils and flavours. Think of it as a pestle and mortar for your drink.

If you don't have a muddler: use a flat-ended rolling pin.

THE LEMON SQUEEZER ⊕

Always, always, always use fresh citrus juices. Never skimp on this part of mixology.

If you don't have a lemon squeezer: use your hands. Roll and squish your fruit on a hard surface, slice in half, and squeeze through your fingers, catching the pips as you go.

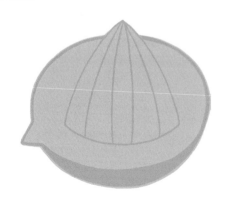

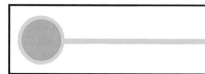

☉ THE SWIZZLE STICK

More than just cocktail furniture, the swizzle allows the drinker to navigate their own drink, stirring as they drink. Great for drinks packed with fruit or garnishes

If you don't have a swizzle stick: use a couple of straws instead.

☉ THE BAR SPOON

The classic bar spoon has a long, twisted handle, a flat end, and a teardrop-shaped spoon used for stirring and measuring out ingredients.

If you don't have a bar spoon: use a sundae or dessert spoon.

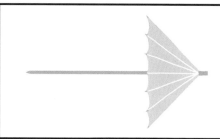

☉ STRAWS, PARASOLS AND PLASTIC MONKEYS

Tricky. Creating hands-down amazing cocktails means that they should look and taste other-worldly just as they are. That's without parasols, plastic monkeys, flashing LED ice cubes and novelty straws you can also wear as glasses. That said, there's something more than a little pleasing about adding the odd frill to your drink. Make sure straws are part of your home bar toolkit – stripy red and white paper ones are pretty eye-catching – and the odd plastic monkey never hurt anyone.

☉ THE COCKTAIL STICK

For spearing cherries, citrus peel, fruit slices, olives, onion slivers, pickles. Sausages, even.

2

GLASSWARE

People make passes at those who use (cocktail) glasses – or however the old adage goes. Steer away from using ordinary glassware to serve drinks, the home mixer should have a little pride in what he presents.

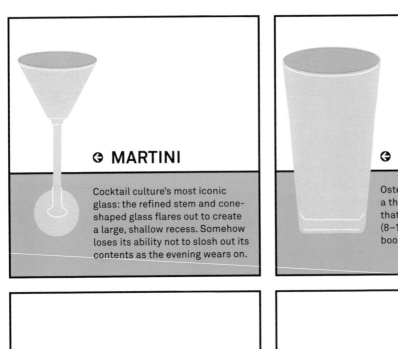

⊖ MARTINI

Cocktail culture's most iconic glass: the refined stem and cone-shaped glass flares out to create a large, shallow recess. Somehow loses its ability not to slosh out its contents as the evening wears on.

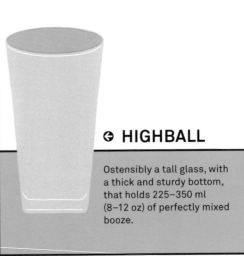

⊖ HIGHBALL

Ostensibly a tall glass, with a thick and sturdy bottom, that holds 225–350 ml (8–12 oz) of perfectly mixed booze.

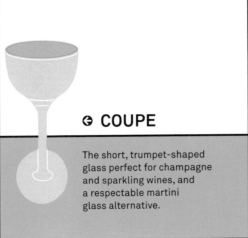

⊖ COUPE

The short, trumpet-shaped glass perfect for champagne and sparkling wines, and a respectable martini glass alternative.

⊖ TUMBLER

The short, straight-sided glass perfect for Old Fashioneds (page 41) or single shot drinks.

⊖ CHAMPAGNE FLUTE

The flute-shaped glass used for Champagne Cocktails (page 50), Bellinis and Mimosas.

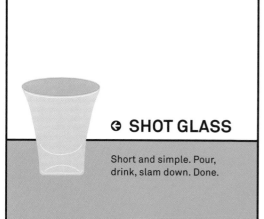

⊖ SHOT GLASS

Short and simple. Pour, drink, slam down. Done.

MOSCOW MULE MUG

The iconic copper mug, traditionally used for a Moscow Mule or Mojito (pages 51 and 73). Packed with ice, it forms a refreshing-looking frosty condensation.

BRANDY SNIFTER

The bulbous-shaped, balloon-like glass with tiny stem used to hold and warm brandies and cognacs.

COLLINS GLASS

The skinny, usually straight-edged version of the Highball.

MARGARITA

The overgrown coupe with ideas above its station. The large rim is built for frosting with salt or sugar.

BOSTON GLASS

The twin brother of the straight-sided pint glass, swapped at birth. Great for mixing in, or using locked into the can of your shaker.

TIKI MUG

The tiki mug was born in mid-century American tiki bars and attributed to Don the Beachcomber, the founding father of tiki culture. It's a tall, wonky-looking ceramic mug with a face like an Easter Island statue.

THE JAM JAR

There are no hard and fast rules for how you serve your drinks – or rather what you serve them in. You can use any number of alternatives: jam jars, tea cups, sciencey test tubes and beakers, Russian tea glasses, to get your guests beyond the pale.

HOW TO
SHAKE IT

Desperate to juggle glasses, flip bottles, light sparklers, and set fire to things? You've opened the wrong book, my friend. This is no hen night. There will be no cream-based drinks (well, maybe a couple). Avoid the dated tricks and tumbles of holiday resort bartending and just focus on making great drinks for you and your friends.

⊙ RIMMING

That's right: rimming.
It's more difficult than it
sounds. Take the Margarita,
for example. Your salted
rim should only stick to the
outside of the glass – and
only reach about half way
around. Add natural sea
salt flakes to a saucer, wet
the rim of your glass with
lime juice, and gently roll
it in salt. Rim your glasses
ahead of time, and place
them back in the fridge to
chill.

Whip out your bar spoon
and your mixing glass
and stir drinks gently and
deftly with ice to chill
the concoction. When
condensation forms on
the outside of the glass,
it's ready to go.

⊙ HOW TO STIR

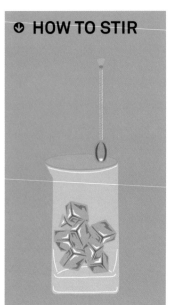

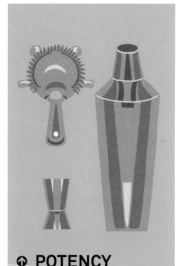

⊙ POTENCY

All cocktails are potent,
but some are more potent
than others. Each drink
should seek to achieve a
perfect balance of flavours,
and can attempt differing
levels of intensity, but
shouldn't get you drunk
(at least not on its own).
Perfect measurements
really matter.

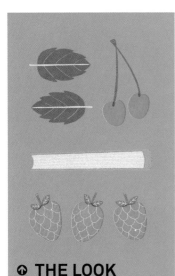

↥ THE LOOK

↧ CHILLING

If you have room, clear a shelf in your freezer and keep your cocktail glasses on ice, or pack them full of ice cubes to chill.

↥ AROMATICS

Fresh garnishes, squeaky clean glasses, clear, filtered-water ice cubes and a perfect balance of colours and visible textures are essential.

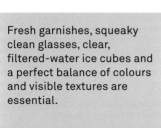

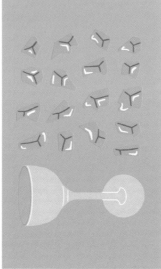

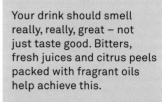

Your drink should smell really, really, great – not just taste good. Bitters, fresh juices and citrus peels packed with fragrant oils help achieve this.

BACK BAR

The Back Bar: think of it as the backbone of your home bar, with a mix of strong, clean and classic spirits, the odd special buy and a few rarities. You don't need to stock up on fine vintage spirits for cocktails – their subtler qualities are lost in the mixing – but you do need to invest in something of quality.

BITTERS

Angostura (the Venezuelan-by-way-of-Trinidad-and-Tobago) bitters are an essential element of the back bar. Said to be a cure for hiccups, the part-herbal, part-alcoholic tincture is highly aromatic, giving cocktails a depth and complexity of taste and colouring white spirits a subtle, sunrise pink. Bitters and cordials producer Fee Brothers (est. 1863) is another good brand to start with: their whisky barrel-aged bitters, rhubarb, and plum flavours are particularly mouth-watering.

CAMPARI AND APEROL

Sharp, ruby red bitters that pep up cocktails and form the basis of the Americano and Negroni (pages 45 and 47) and are really quite life-changing mixed with soda water and sparkling wine.

GIN

Artisanal gins packed with unique infusions of acrid juniper berries and herbs are worth investing in. But for a clean, crisp and subtle flavour, Bombay Sapphire, Tanqueray, Hendrick's and Plymouth are all reliable brands.

CASSIS

Invest in a good-quality crème de cassis or crème de mûre: dark berry-flavoured liqueurs for Kirs and Kir Royales and more besides.

VERMOUTH

The fortified wine packed with botanicals, in sweet or dry versions. Get both and keep them refrigerated after opening.

RUM

Rum is the liquor sailors drink to ward off scurvy. Cheap rum, that is. Invest a little in an upscale number such as Zacapa or Brugal Anejo.

TEQUILA

The agave-based brain melter. Unaged (or aged for no more than 60 days in steel containers), silver (blanco) tequila is an essential part of your back bar. Tequila gold is sweet and smooth, *reposado* ('rested') tequila, is smoky, aged in wood-lined barrels.

BRANDY

VSOP cognac and calvados are perfectly respectable brands for your back bar, anything classier should be enjoyed without mixing.

WHISKY

Pick a sturdy, deep-tasting bourbon rather than an aged malt. Monkey Shoulder, Knob Creek and Bullet are all strong contenders.

VODKA

Stolichnaya, Smirnoff and Absolut are all reliable brands, while the more expensive Crystal Head vodka – encased in a skull-shaped bottle – certainly looks the part.

OTHER ESSENTIALS

Hardly anyone uses cola as a mixer any more. Make sure you have a ginger beer or ale, sparkling water, prosecco, cava or champagne, and freshly squeezed citrus juices, coconut water and – always – a truckload of ice.

Rarities
Maraschino cherries, Hibiscus flowers in syrup Homemade syrups, Grenadine, Olives and pickles and Tomato juice.

5

SYRUPS, BRINES
AND SOURS

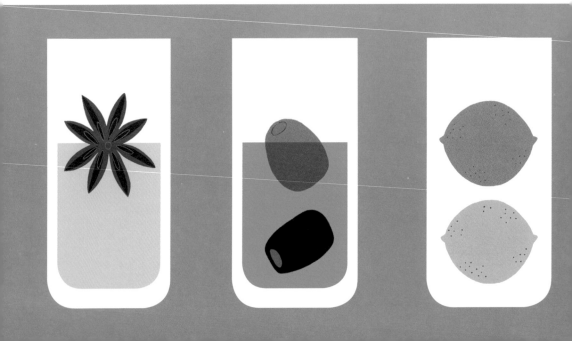

The boozy trinity: syrups, brines and sours are the warheads in the home mixer's arsenal. Syrups sweeten it down, sours sharpen it up, and brines slip in a pickle.

SYRUP

The sweet stuff. Taking the edge off sour citrus flavours and softening the taste of bitter spirits, a dash of sugar syrup can transform a drink, turning the toughest liquor into soda pop. Flavoured syrup adds a level of complexity a fresh ingredient just can't achieve. And it's very nearly foolproof to make – start with the simple syrup recipe, graduate to the flavoured infusions, then start to create your own. You could always buy syrup ready-made, but it's so simple, you really don't need to.

It's not essential to use unrefined sugar, but it's tastier, chemical-free and – used in all your cocktail recipes and syrup-making – lends a wobbly irregularity to proceedings that could only be handmade.

SIMPLE SYRUP

Makes enough dashes for about 15 drinks

Ingredients
200 ml (7 oz) water
100 g (3½ oz) Demerara (turbinado),
cane or granulated (raw) sugar
1 tablespoon corn syrup (optional)

Equipment
non-stick saucepan
wooden spoon
funnel

Glass
200 ml (7 oz) kilner jar, sterilised
glass bottle with stopper, sterilised

Method
Boil the water and gently add the sugar. Reduce the heat and stir constantly for 3–5 minutes, until all the sugar is dissolved and the syrup is clear. Turn off the heat and leave to cool. Adding a spoonful of corn syrup to the cooled mixture will help keep the syrup smooth. When still runny, funnel into a kilner jar or a glass bottle with stopper. Store in the fridge for up to six weeks.

BROWN SUGAR SYRUP

Makes enough dashes for about 15 drinks

Ingredients
200ml (7 oz) water
100g (3½ oz) dark brown sugar
1 tablespoon freshly grated ginger
1 tablespoon corn syrup (optional)

Equipment
non-stick saucepan
heatproof bowl
wooden spoon
funnel
cheesecloth

Glass
200 ml (7 oz) kilner jar, sterilised
glass bottle with stopper, sterilised

Method
Boil the water and gently add the sugar and ginger. Reduce the heat and stir constantly for 3–5 minutes, until all the sugar is dissolved. Turn off the heat and leave to cool for 20–30 minutes for the flavours to infuse. Adding a spoonful of corn syrup to the cooled mixture will help keep the syrup smooth. When still runny, pass through a cheesecloth-lined strainer into a heatproof bowl then decant into a kilner jar or funnel into a glass bottle with stopper. Store in the fridge for up to six weeks.

RHUBARB, GINGER & STAR ANISE SYRUP

Makes enough dashes for about 15 drinks

Ingredients
200 ml (7 oz) water
100 g (3½ oz) Demerara (turbinado), cane or granulated (raw) sugar
2 rhubarb stalks, cut into chunks
1 tablespoon freshly grated ginger
1 star anise, slightly crushed
dash of lemon juice, freshly squeezed
1 tablespoon corn syrup (optional)

Equipment
non-stick saucepan
heatproof bowl
wooden spoon
funnel
cheesecloth

Glass
200 ml (7 oz) kilner jar, sterilised
glass bottle with stopper, sterilised

Method
Boil the water and gently add the sugar, rhubarb, ginger, star anise and lemon juice. Reduce the heat and stir constantly for 3–5 minutes, until all the sugar is dissolved. Turn off the heat and leave to cool for 20–30 minutes for the flavours to infuse. Adding a spoonful of corn syrup will help keep the mixture smooth. When still runny, pass through a cheesecloth-lined strainer into a heatproof bowl then decant into a kilner jar or funnel into a glass bottle with stopper. Store in the fridge for up to six weeks.

TEQUILA AND VODKA INFUSIONS

Ingredients
200ml (7 oz) vodka or tequila
5 teaspoons freshly ground black pepper

Equipment
wooden spoon, funnel, cheesecloth

Glass
200 ml (7 oz) kilner jar, sterilised
glass bottle with stopper, sterilised

Method
Steep your spirit with the pepper, seal and infuse at room temperature for 7 days, stirring occasionally. After 7 days, strain through the cheesecloth and funnel into the bottle.

OR TRY THESE INFUSIONS

Using Simple Syrup (page 32) as your base, add your own infusions, tweaking amounts to taste, according to how potent your flavourings are. A sprig or two for rosemary syrup should do it, whereas mint or basil syrups – because the leaves are more fragile – require a good handful. It's not an exact science.

Brown Sugar & Molasses
Ginger & Cardamom
Basil & Lime
Mint
Rosemary
Sage
Ground Coffee
Pink Peppercorn
Vanilla Bean

BRINES

Brines: odd, salty infusions stolen from olive, caper and pickle jars add a savoury, acid kick to a drink, cutting through sweetness with more brute strength than citrus. But adding brine to an already hard, sharp liquor almost underlines its power. Olive brine mixed with a gin or vodka martini lends a deep, savoury kick; cocktail onions and a drop of vinegar add a sharp, acrid note; while a drop of pickle juice in a shot of rye whisky seems only to increase its firepower, adding an undeniable tang. The best bit? It's like having a drink and dinner in one, which – frankly – allows time for more drinking.

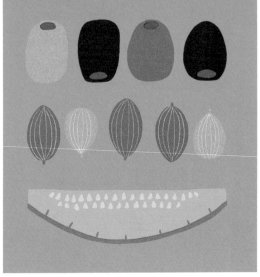

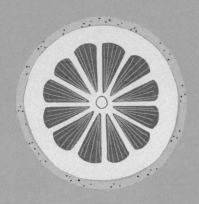

SOURS

Sours – a citrus-based mix that can include sugar syrup and egg white – cut through the gloopy sweetness of liqueurs. Shaken up with egg white and sugar syrup, a hit of fresh lemon and lime juice, or grapefruit and blood orange forms the fizzing topnote of recipes such as the Whisky Sour (page 44). But a simple half-measure of lemon juice stirred through a glass of Amaretto on the rocks will also do the trick, turning a nanna's snifter into man fuel.

SIMPLE SOUR MIX

Ingredients
1 tablespoon lemon juice, freshly squeezed
1 tablespoon lime juice, freshly squeezed

Method
Mix both juices and deploy.

CLASSIC SOUR MIX

Ingredients
1 tablespoon lemon juice, freshly squeezed
1 tablespoon lime juice, freshly squeezed
1 tablespoon Simple Syrup (page 32)
1 egg white

Method
Mix both juices, the syrup and egg white and shake over ice with your chosen spirit.

BLOODY SOUR MIX

Ingredients
1 tablespoon blood orange juice,
    freshly squeezed
1 tablespoon pink grapefruit juice,
    freshly squeezed

Method
Mix both juices and deploy.

Part Two: THE COCKTAIL LIST

6

THE
CLASSICS

Cocktail culture's greatest hits, the classics should be the first drinks a mixer masters. You can hone them at home to professional mixologist levels and they are all safe bets to order every time you are in a cocktail bar, without even flicking through the menu.

MARTINI

❶ INGREDIENTS

50 ML (2 OZ) DRY GIN
1 TEASPOON DRY VERMOUTH
COCKTAIL OLIVE, TO GARNISH

❷ EQUIPMENT

MARTINI
OR COUPE

SHAKER OR
MIXING GLASS

BAR SPOON

The world's most well-known cocktail is perhaps the simplest and easiest to master. Chill the glass, use a high-quality gin – packed with herbs and juniper notes – and serve ice-cold.

❸ METHOD

Shake or stir the gin and vermouth with ice cubes, then strain into a martini glass or coupe. Garnish with a cocktail olive.

OLD FASHIONED

❶ INGREDIENTS

1 UNREFINED SUGAR CUBE • 2 DASHES OF
ANGOSTURA BITTERS • 1 TABLESPOON SODA WATER
50 ML (2 OZ) BOURBON • TWIST OF ORANGE PEEL
MARASCHINO CHERRY, TO GARNISH

❷ EQUIPMENT

TUMBLER   MUDDLER

Bourbon, disguised with sugar and
bitters and loosened up with a dash
of soda. A large twist of orange peel,
left sticking out of the Old Fashioned
like a middle finger, rubs aromatically
against the nose as you sip.

❸ METHOD

Dissolve the sugar cube in the bitters, soda
water and bourbon in a tumbler. Muddle with
a twist of orange peel, add two large cubes of
ice and a maraschino cherry to garnish.

COSMOPOLITAN

❶ INGREDIENTS

50 ML (2 OZ) VODKA
25 ML (1 OZ) TRIPLE SEC
25 ML (1 OZ) CRANBERRY JUICE
TWIST OF ORANGE PEEL, TO GARNISH

❷ EQUIPMENT

MARTINI
OR COUPE

SHAKER

Remember the '90s? This pink, sharp, vodka-based cocktail dominated the upscale drinkeries of New York, London and beyond, getting all manner of bright young hen-nighters drunk in the process. The Cosmo may have drifted out of the spotlight, but it's still a classic.

❸ METHOD

Shake the ingredients with ice cubes and strain into a chilled martini glass or coupe, garnish with orange peel and serve.

LONG ISLAND ICED TEA

❶ INGREDIENTS

25 ML (1 OZ) VODKA • 25 ML (1 OZ) GIN
25 ML (1 OZ) LIGHT RUM • 25 ML (1 OZ) TEQUILA
25 ML (1 OZ) LEMON JUICE, FRESHLY SQUEEZED
25 ML (1 OZ) ORANGE LIQUEUR • 1 TEASPOON CASTER
(SUPERFINE) SUGAR • SLICE OF LEMON, TO GARNISH
SLICE OF LIME, TO GARNISH

❷ EQUIPMENT

HIGHBALL   BAR SPOON   SWIZZLE STICK,
                         STRAWS

A cup of hot tea and a little drop of vodka just seems, well, dirty. Throw out the tea and add a bucket of alcohol and you apparently have yourself a rather classy, artful drink.

❸ METHOD

Pour the ingredients into a highball glass filled with ice cubes, stir and add the lemon and lime slices. Serve with a swizzle stick and 2 straws.

GIN RICKEY

Simple, sharp, refreshing and – after a couple – dizzying. Tweak the balance between sugar and lime to taste, but a good Rickey should be bright, sharp and strong.

① INGREDIENTS ⋯⋯

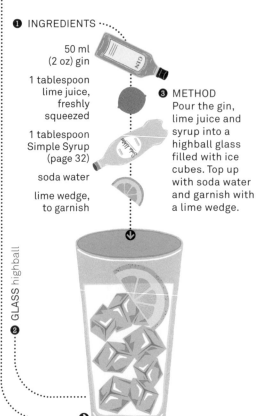

50 ml (2 oz) gin

1 tablespoon lime juice, freshly squeezed

1 tablespoon Simple Syrup (page 32)

soda water

lime wedge, to garnish

③ METHOD
Pour the gin, lime juice and syrup into a highball glass filled with ice cubes. Top up with soda water and garnish with a lime wedge.

② GLASS highball

WHISKEY SOUR

Citrus and sugar syrup – the perfect 50/50 Sour mix – muddied with bourbon, cherry juice and two dashes of Angostura.

① INGREDIENTS ⋯⋯

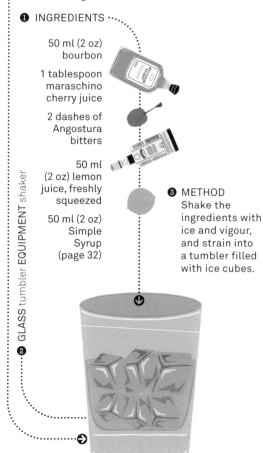

50 ml (2 oz) bourbon

1 tablespoon maraschino cherry juice

2 dashes of Angostura bitters

50 ml (2 oz) lemon juice, freshly squeezed

50 ml (2 oz) Simple Syrup (page 32)

③ METHOD
Shake the ingredients with ice and vigour, and strain into a tumbler filled with ice cubes.

② GLASS tumbler **EQUIPMENT** shaker

ROB ROY

A drink inspired by the Scots hero, with a healthy amount of Scotch and a surprise cherry garnish. Like a sporran, soaked in a teapot.

GLASS martini or coupe EQUIPMENT mixing glass, bar spoon

❶ INGREDIENTS

25 ml (1 oz) vodka

50 ml (2 oz) Scotch whisky

40 ml (1½ oz) sweet vermouth

4 dashes of Angostura bitters

orange peel, to garnish

maraschino cherry, to garnish

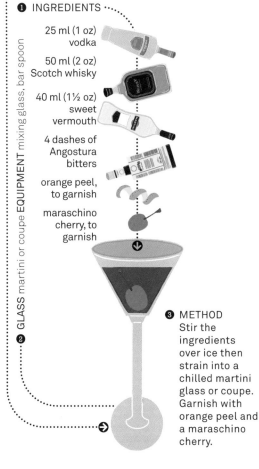

❸ METHOD
Stir the ingredients over ice then strain into a chilled martini glass or coupe. Garnish with orange peel and a maraschino cherry.

AMERICANO

This Italian mainstay is a bitter, aromatic cocktail classic. Sweet vermouth does a little to soften its edges and the deep red hue adds a bit of drama – if that's your thing.

GLASS highball or tumbler

❶ INGREDIENTS

25 ml (1 oz) Campari

25 ml (1 oz) sweet vermouth

soda water

slice of orange, to garnish

❸ METHOD
Pour the spirits over ice cubes and top with soda water. Choose a highball for a subtler drink, or a tumbler for a punchy finish. Garnish with a slice of orange.

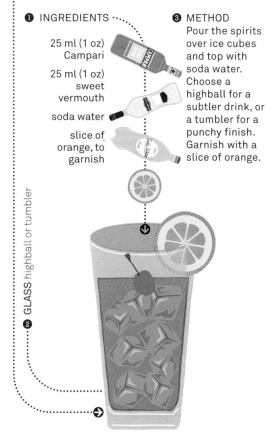

SINGAPORE SLING

❶ INGREDIENTS

50 ML (2 OZ) GIN • 25 ML (1 OZ) CHERRY BRANDY
50 ML (2 OZ) LEMON JUICE, FRESHLY SQUEEZED
1 TEASPOON GRENADINE • SODA WATER
MARASCHINO CHERRY, TO GARNISH

❷ EQUIPMENT

TUMBLER   SHAKER

The design of a barman at Raffles, Singapore in the early 1900s, and a reworking of the classic Gin Sling, the Singapore Sling is a deep pink, cherry-infused gin cocktail, served long.

❸ METHOD

Shake the gin, cherry brandy, lemon juice and grenadine with ice and vigour. Strain into a tumbler over ice cubes, top with soda and add a maraschino cherry to garnish.

NEGRONI

❶ INGREDIENTS

25 ML (1 OZ) DRY GIN
25 ML (1 OZ) SWEET VERMOUTH
50 ML (2 OZ) CAMPARI
TWIST OF ORANGE PEEL, TO GARNISH

❷ EQUIPMENT

| TUMBLER | MIXING GLASS | BAR SPOON | STRAINER |

The tougher, more intense version of the Americano, created in Florence where a hero of the cocktail world thought to replace soda water with gin. What a marvellous man!

❸ METHOD

Stir the ingredients in a mixing glass over ice. Strain into a tumbler filled with ice cubes. Garnish with the orange peel.

MANHATTAN

Simple, strong and more than a little elegant, the Manhattan is as iconic as the NYC borough in which it was created, only with less attitude.

❶ INGREDIENTS

75 ML (2½ OZ) BOURBON
25 ML (1 OZ) SWEET VERMOUTH
2 DASHES OF ANGOSTURA BITTERS • MARASCHINO
CHERRY OR A TWIST OF LEMON PEEL, TO GARNISH

❷ EQUIPMENT

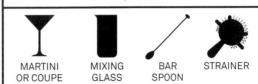

MARTINI OR COUPE · MIXING GLASS · BAR SPOON · STRAINER

❸ METHOD

Stir the ingredients in a mixing glass over ice. Strain into a chilled martini glass or coupe. Garnish with a maraschino cherry or a twist of lemon peel.

GIMLET

❶ INGREDIENTS

50 ML (2 OZ) DRY GIN
10 ML (⅓ OZ) LIME JUICE,
FRESHLY SQUEEZED

❷ EQUIPMENT

MARTINI
OR COUPE

SHAKER

❸ METHOD

The original gin and juice – a power-punch of a cocktail, you can swap the lime juice for any other acidic fruit.

Shake the ingredients with ice and vigour and strain into a chilled martini glass or coupe with a couple of ice cubes.

CHAMPAGNE COCKTAIL

❶ INGREDIENTS

1 UNREFINED SUGAR CUBE
2 DASHES OF ANGOSTURA BITTERS
25 ML (1 OZ) BRANDY
90 ML (3 OZ) CHAMPAGNE

❷ EQUIPMENT

CHAMPAGNE
FLUTE

❸ METHOD

There's little more decadent than considering champagne a mixer – but this brandy-based cocktail does just that. Pepped up with a sugar cube and Angostura bitters; for special decadence-based occasions only.

Place the sugar in the bottom of the champagne flute, add the dashes of Angostura bitters, then the brandy and top with the chilled champagne.

MOSCOW MULE

❶ INGREDIENTS

½ A LIME
50 ML (2 OZ) VODKA
100 ML (3½ OZ) GINGER BEER

❷ EQUIPMENT

MOSCOW MULE MUG
OR TALL GLASS

The Mule. The ass-end of the equestrian world, the mule's humble power and mangy countenance inspired this cocktail, a sort of tribute to the world's hardest working not-horse.

❸ METHOD

Squeeze the lime – with all your might – into a Moscow Mule mug or tall glass, add the used lime rind, three ice cubes, top with ginger beer and stir.

PUNCH DRUNK

Why mix one drink for each guest when you can make one giant one and invite them to dip in? Such is the philosophy of punch. Use a proper cut-crystal punch bowl, a pitcher or bucket, upturned top hat, slipper, saucepan or dog bowl. Punches: it's time to throw some.

BROOKLYN DROPOUT

The swoopy fringed, inked and mustachioed of Brooklyn gather in their backyards on a hot summers' night, talk through their latest vegan baking blog idea and dip vintage tea cups into a pitcher full of this amazing punch. But don't let that put you off – it's delicious.

Ingredients
2 bottles of champagne (750ml/25 oz each)
950 ml (32 oz) ginger beer
25 ml (1 oz) lemon juice, freshly squeezed
50 ml (2 oz) elderflower liqueur
dash of Angostura bitters
slices of lime, to garnish
slices of peach, to garnish

Equipment
punch bowl, ladle or small jug

Glass
tumblers or paper cups

Method
Add an ice block or ring (page 15) to a punch bowl, pour in the ingredients and stir. Drop in lime and peach slices to garnish.

WATERMELON RUM PUNCH

Super-fresh watermelon – pulped into submission – mint syrup and lemonade sweeten up this eye-wateringly strong punch. A bright pink, summery slap in the face.

Ingredients
1 watermelon, peeled, sliced and deseeded
950 ml (32 oz) white rum
280 ml (9½ oz) tequila
25 ml (1 oz) Mint Syrup (see page 34)
25 ml (1 oz) lime juice, freshly squeezed
1 large bottle (2 litres/68 oz) of lemonade
50g (2 oz) mint leaves, ripped, to garnish
slices of lime, to garnish
slices of watermelon, to garnish

Equipment
blender, punch bowl, ladle or small jug

Glass
tumblers or paper cups

Method
Pulp the sliced watermelon in a blender. Add an ice block or ring (page 15) to a punch bowl, pour in all the ingredients and stir. Drop in the mint, lime and watermelon slices to garnish. Add more Mint Syrup to taste.

ST PETERSBURGER PUNCH

Punch isn't always for sharing: this Russian-themed punch for one uses Russian vodka, crème de cassis, fresh raspberries, a champagne top and a steely reserve.

Ingredients
50 ml (2 oz) Russian vodka
50 ml (2 oz) lemon juice, freshly squeezed
25 ml (1 oz) crème de cassis
25 ml (1 oz) fresh raspberry purée
dash of raspberry liqueur
dash of Simple Syrup (page 32)
champagne, to top

Equipment
shaker

Glass
highball

Method
Shake the vodka, lemon juice, crème de cassis, raspberry purée, raspberry liqueur and syrup with ice cubes and vigour. Strain into a highball glass filled with crushed ice and top with champagne.

ALMOST CLASSIC SANGRIA

The taste of Spanish summer holidays, this red wine-based fruity punch seems to get stronger and stronger as the evening progresses. I've given the 'classic' recipe a little contemporary tweak – swapping orange slices for fat wedges of blood orange.

Ingredients
1 bottle (750ml/25 oz) of red wine
1 large bottle (2 litres/68 oz) of lemonade
100 ml (3½ oz) orange juice, freshly squeezed
blood orange wedges
small bunch of mint, leaves torn

Equipment
punch bowl, ladle or small jug

Glass
tumblers

Method
Add an ice block or ring (page 15) to a punch bowl, pour in the ingredients and stir. Let the flavours infuse for about 20 minutes, adding more orange juice to taste.

HONEY BEER PUNCH

A sweet, beery take on Long Island Iced Tea with gin, honey and a premium brew creating a slip-down punch for one. Add more honey to taste.

Ingredients
1 teaspoon honey
splash of hot water
15 ml (½ oz) lemon juice, freshly squeezed
50 ml (2 oz) gin
chilled premium beer, to top
slice of lemon, to garnish

Equipment
kettle, mixing glass, bar spoon

Glass
tall

Method
Melt a generous teaspoon of honey in a mixing glass with a splash of hot water and allow to cool. Add to a tall glass filled with ice cubes, lemon juice and gin. Top with chilled beer, add a lemon slice to garnish.

BEER TEA

Start the morning with a strong cup of tea, have another eight or so to get you through the day and switch to beer in the evening. Why not do it all in one drink? Mixing this punch is mind-numbingly easy – and supremely tasty. Use a good-quality tea and an excellent beer.

Ingredients
6 bottles of premium beer (330 ml/11½ oz each)
950 ml (32 oz) ginger beer
950 ml (32 oz) cold, strong English Breakfast tea
slices of orange, to garnish
50g mint leaves, ripped, to garnish

Equipment
punch bowl, ladle or small jug

Glass
tumblers or paper cups

Method
Add an ice block or ring (page 15) to a punch bowl, pour in the ingredients and stir. Drop in orange slices and mint to garnish.

PLANTER'S PUNCH

The classic one-cup punch with dark rum softened with sugar syrup and Angostura bitters and freshened up with ice-cold soda and lime. Add more sugar syrup to taste. A cocktail classic.

Ingredients
50 ml (2 oz) dark rum
25 ml (1 oz) lime juice, freshly squeezed
2 dashes of Angostura bitters
dash of Simple Syrup (page 32)
soda water
lime wedge, to garnish

Equipment
shaker

Glass
highball

Method
Shake the rum, lime juice, Angostura bitters and syrup over ice. Strain into a highball glass filled with crushed ice. Top up with soda water and garnish with a lime wedge.

POOR MAN'S CHAMPAGNE PUNCH

Not quite pay day? Don't have a spare case of Moët in the chiller? Be rich in spirit with this poor man's punch that swaps champagne for beer and hides the dirty deed under a bushel of frozen raspberries and ice-cold vodka.

Ingredients
100 g (3½ oz) frozen raspberries,
   plus extra to garnish
25 ml (1 oz) lime juice, freshly squeezed
25 ml (1 oz) Simple Syrup (page 32)
280 ml (9½ oz) vodka
4 bottles of chilled premium beer (330 ml/
   11½ oz each)
slices of lime, to garnish

Equipment
blender

Glass
punch bowl

Method
Blend the frozen raspberries, lime juice and sugar syrup then add to a punch bowl with the vodka and chilled beer. Add lime slices and frozen whole raspberries to garnish.

BEST IN SHOW

Sometimes a drink just resounds. You take your first sip, love it, and you can't quite explain why. Perhaps it's a particular subtlety of taste that reminds you of a time, a place, or a person, or perhaps it's the environment you find yourself in when you drain your first glass and slam it down on the table. It just does something to you: it's your Best In Show.

ROSITA

❶ INGREDIENTS

50 ML (2 OZ) AGED TEQUILA • 25 ML (1 OZ) SWEET VERMOUTH • 25 ML (1 OZ) DRY VERMOUTH
25 ML (1 OZ) APEROL • DASH OF ANGOSTURA BITTERS
ORANGE PEEL, TO GARNISH

❷ EQUIPMENT

MARTINI OR COUPE   SHAKER

❸ METHOD

The ruby red, rather potent Rosita has many versions, but this is considered the purest. Use an aged (*reposado*) tequila for extra smoky authenticity, and don't scrimp on the peel.

Shake the tequila, vermouths, Aperol and Angostura bitters with ice cubes and vigour, pour into a chilled martini glass or coupe and garnish with orange peel.

APPLE CATCHER

❶ INGREDIENTS

50 ML (2 OZ) APPLE BRANDY
25 ML (1 OZ) ORANGE JUICE, FRESHLY SQUEEZED
1 TABLESPOON LEMON JUICE, FRESHLY SQUEEZED
1 TABLESPOON PURE MAPLE SYRUP
LEMON PEEL, TO GARNISH

❷ EQUIPMENT

TUMBLER   SHAKER

❸ METHOD

Apple brandy, cut through with sharp citrus and a woody, maple syrup depth. Golden and delicious.

Shake the apple brandy, orange and lemon juices and maple syrup with ice cubes and vigour. Strain into a tumbler filled with a large piece of ice and garnish with lemon peel.

SPARTACUS

❶ INGREDIENTS

25 ML (1 OZ) SCOTCH WHISKY
25 ML (1 OZ) ORANGE JUICE, FRESHLY SQUEEZED
22 ML (¾ OZ) SWEET VERMOUTH
22 ML (¾ OZ) CHERRY HEERING
MARASCHINO CHERRY, TO GARNISH

❷ EQUIPMENT

TUMBLER   SHAKER

❸ METHOD

It is said Scotch – good Scotch – should only be mixed with ice or soda. And here's Spartacus, getting friendly with orange juice, Cherry Heering liqueur and sweet vermouth. And all the better for it.

Shake the Scotch, orange juice, vermouth and Cherry Heering with ice cubes and vigour and strain into a tumbler with a large piece of ice. Drop in a cherry to garnish.

TAKE IVY

❶ INGREDIENTS

50 ML (2 OZ) GIN • DASH OF ORANGE BITTERS
22 ML (¾ OZ) PORT • ORANGE PEEL, TO GARNISH

❷ EQUIPMENT

MARTINI OR COUPE   SHAKER

❸ METHOD

A collegiate, on-campus classic. While others are fashioning beer bongs and attempting keg stands, you can delicately sip a Take Ivy: a gin, port and bitters cocktail with class.

Shake the gin and bitters with ice cubes and vigour and strain into a chilled martini glass or coupe. Pour the port gently down the side of the glass so it sinks underneath. Garnish with orange peel perched on the rim (not the in the drink) and serve.

ESPRESSO MARTINI

Slowly, but thankfully, stimulation drinks are winging their way off the modern cocktail list and the originals are being rediscovered. With its keep-awake qualities, the Espresso Martini will knock your socks off. Even if you're not wearing any.

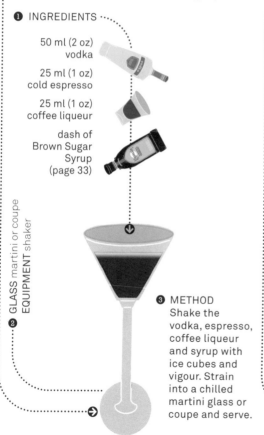

❶ INGREDIENTS

50 ml (2 oz)
vodka

25 ml (1 oz)
cold espresso

25 ml (1 oz)
coffee liqueur

dash of
Brown Sugar
Syrup
(page 33)

GLASS martini or coupe
EQUIPMENT shaker

❷

❸ METHOD
Shake the vodka, espresso, coffee liqueur and syrup with ice cubes and vigour. Strain into a chilled martini glass or coupe and serve.

HOLY WATER

A powerful long drink, freshened up with tonic and grenadine. Named for the nuns who find it the perfect pick-me-up after prayer time.

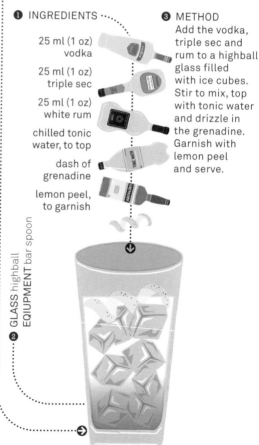

❶ INGREDIENTS

25 ml (1 oz)
vodka

25 ml (1 oz)
triple sec

25 ml (1 oz)
white rum

chilled tonic
water, to top

dash of
grenadine

lemon peel,
to garnish

❸ METHOD
Add the vodka, triple sec and rum to a highball glass filled with ice cubes. Stir to mix, top with tonic water and drizzle in the grenadine. Garnish with lemon peel and serve.

GLASS highball
EQUIPMENT bar spoon

❷

MAXIM

The musky, manly way to drink crème de cacao, toughened up with dry vermouth gin, and topped off with a slightly ironic cherry.

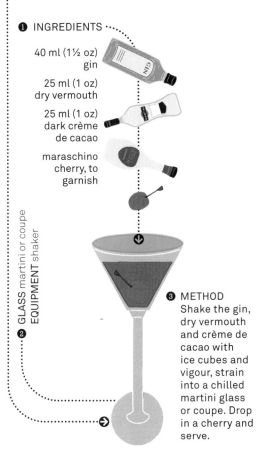

1 INGREDIENTS

40 ml (1½ oz) gin

25 ml (1 oz) dry vermouth

25 ml (1 oz) dark crème de cacao

maraschino cherry, to garnish

2 GLASS martini or coupe
EQUIPMENT shaker

3 METHOD
Shake the gin, dry vermouth and crème de cacao with ice cubes and vigour, strain into a chilled martini glass or coupe. Drop in a cherry and serve.

THE SLAMMER

Some drinks are for sipping, others are for slamming. Tequila, crème de cacao and a splash of champagne in a tough tumbler, slammed noisily and chucked down your neck.

1 INGREDIENTS

50 ml (2 oz) tequila gold

50 ml (2 oz) champagne

dash of crème de cacao

3 METHOD
Pour the tequila, champagne and crème de cacao into a tumbler. Cover with your hand, slam down on a hard surface then drink in one.

2 GLASS tumbler

SOUR FIZZ

❶ INGREDIENTS

40 ML (1½ OZ) TEQUILA GOLD • 25 ML (1 OZ) LIME JUICE, FRESHLY SQUEEZED • 25 ML (1 OZ) RUNNY HONEY 5 DASHES OF ORANGE BITTERS • BITTER LEMON, TO TOP SLICE OF LEMON, TO GARNISH

❷ EQUIPMENT

HIGHBALL   SHAKER

With an equal balance of honey and lime juice at its base, a punch of tequila gold, and a tickle of orange bitters, the Sour Fizz draws its tangy qualities from a top of bitter lemon.

❸ METHOD

Shake the tequila, lime juice, honey and bitters with ice and vigour, then pour into a highball filled with ice cubes. Top with bitter lemon, garnish with a lemon slice and serve.

DIRTY DICK

❶ INGREDIENTS

25 ML (1 OZ) TEQUILA GOLD
25 ML (1 OZ) BLACK PEPPER VODKA
25 ML (1 OZ) LIME JUICE, FRESHLY SQUEEZED
2–3 TEASPOONS CAPER BERRY BRINE
CAPER BERRY, TO GARNISH

❷ EQUIPMENT

MARTINI OR COUPE   SHAKER

❸ METHOD

Shake the tequila, vodka, lime juice and brine over ice. Strain into a chilled martini glass or coupe, drop in a caper berry to garnish and serve.

The filthy-sounding name refers to the caper berry brine that muddies up this fiery, powerful drink with a salty, fruity aspect. Otherwise, the Dick is really a tequila and black pepper vodka version of the dirty martini. Despite its name, the Dirty Dick is surprisingly fragrant.

CLASS ACT

❶ INGREDIENTS

1 UNREFINED SUGAR CUBE
5 DASHES OF ANGOSTURA BITTERS
25 ML (1 OZ) GRAND MARNIER
CHILLED CHAMPAGNE, TO TOP
ORANGE PEEL, TO GARNISH

❷ EQUIPMENT

CHAMPAGNE
FLUTE

❸ METHOD

Running with the wrong crowd? Finding
your friends a little rough around the edges?
Serve them the Class Act – a Grand Marnier-
infused champagne cocktail – and see them
dumbfounded by its poshness.

Soak the sugar cube in the bitters, add
to the glass and cover with Grand Marnier.
Top with chilled champagne and garnish
with orange peel.

RUDOLPH

50 ML (2 OZ) GIN
25 ML (1 OZ) ELDERFLOWER LIQUEUR
CHAMPAGNE, TO TOP
STRING OF FRESH REDCURRANTS, TO GARNISH

② EQUIPMENT

MARTINI, CHAMPAGNE
FLUTE OR COUPE

③ METHOD

Gin, elderflower and chilled champagne:
a perfect festive season cocktail, with a
string of Rudolph noses for added schmaltz.
Looks great in a martini glass, coupe
or champagne flute.

Pour the gin and elderflower liqueur
into a chilled martini glass, champagne flute
or coupe, top with champagne and garnish
with a string of fresh redcurrants.

TROPICAL
AND TIKI

Cocktail umbrellas, sparklers, swizzle sticks, palm fronds ... Tropical and Tiki cocktails require a complete suspension of taste, replacing it with a love of exotic trimmings and fruity blends. Underneath the frills and sweetness lie powerful, knock-out cocktails.

PINA COLADA

❶ INGREDIENTS

50 ML (2 OZ) WHITE RUM
25 ML (1 OZ) DARK RUM
75 ML (2½ OZ) PINEAPPLE JUICE
50 ML (2 OZ) COCONUT CREAM
PINEAPPLE WEDGES, TO GARNISH

❷ EQUIPMENT

HIGHBALL   BLENDER

The most tropical of all the tropical drinks. Mixed correctly, the Pina Colada is the taste equivalent of waking up on a tropical beach. Naked. And without your wallet.

❸ METHOD

Crush ice in a blender, then add the white and dark rum, pineapple juice and coconut cream and blend until smooth. Pour into a highball glass and garnish with pineapple wedges.

MOJITO

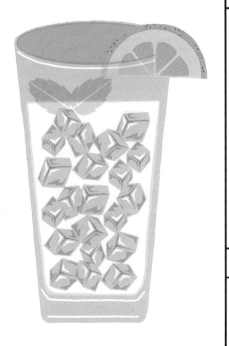

❶ INGREDIENTS

50 ML (2 OZ) LIME JUICE, FRESHLY SQUEEZED
2 HEAPED TEASPOONS UNREFINED SUGAR
HANDFUL OF MINT • 75 ML (2½ OZ) LIGHT RUM
SODA WATER, TO TOP

❷ EQUIPMENT

HIGHBALL

MUDDLER

TEASPOON

Ernest Hemingway's favourite Cuban tipple,
the Mojito is simple in construction.
Add more sugar for a less grown-up taste.

❸ METHOD

Add the lime juice, sugar and most of the mint
leaves to a highball glass and muddle. Add
rum, fill with crushed ice, top with soda and
garnish with a sprig of mint.

PEACH & BLACK PEPPER MARGARITA

Like the devil, the Margarita has many forms. This peach and pepper version can be as sweet or as spicy as you like. Use your own infused tequila (page 34) and adjust the peach schnapps to taste – this drink should be sour and peppery rather than sickly sweet.

❶ INGREDIENTS

handful of sea salt flakes
3 teaspoons freshly crushed black pepper
1 tablespoon lime juice, freshly squeezed, wedge retained
1 large ripe peach
50 ml (2 oz) black pepper infused tequila
25 ml (1 oz) peach schnapps

❷ EQUIPMENT

MARTINI OR COUPE   PESTLE AND MORTAR   BLENDER

❸ METHOD

Crush the salt flakes and pepper in a pestle and mortar, run a squeezed-out lime wedge around the outside of a chilled martini glass or coupe and roll gently through the salt to cover half the glass, keeping it on the outside only. Stone a large ripe peach, cut into chunks and add to a blender with ice cubes, the black pepper tequila, peach schnapps and lime juice. Strain into a martini glass or coupe.

TEQUILA POMEGRANATE

Let the layers of this tall drink sit separately, allowing the drinker to twizzle them into a blend. The orange liqueur and lime cut through the tequila and then topped with sweet pomegranate juice.

Ingredients
50 ml (2 oz) tequila
25 ml (1 oz) Cointreau
1 tablespoon lime juice, freshly squeezed
pomegranate juice, to top
slice of lime, to garnish

Glass
highball

Equipment
swizzle stick

Method
Pour the tequila, Cointreau and lime juice into a highball glass over crushed ice, top with pomegranate juice, add a swizzle stick and lime slice, to garnish.

BANANA DAIQUIRI

The classic Tiki recipe... and probably the most camp. The dark rum adds a caramelised note to the banana flavour and the lime cuts through the sweetness.

Ingredients
50 ml (2 oz) chilled water
50 ml (2 oz) dark rum
25 ml (1 oz) banana liqueur
1 tablespoon lime juice, freshly squeezed
dash of Simple Syrup (page 32)
1 very ripe banana, plus a slice to garnish

Glass
highball

Equipment
blender

Method
Add the water, rum, banana liqueur, lime juice, syrup and banana to a blender with ice cubes. Purée until smooth. Pour into a highball glass over crushed ice. Garnish with a banana slice.

BEACH HOUSE

❶ INGREDIENTS

50 ML (2 OZ) GIN
1 TABLESPOON LIME JUICE, FRESHLY SQUEEZED
COCONUT WATER, TO TOP
SLICE OF LIME, TO GARNISH

❷ EQUIPMENT

HIGHBALL   SWIZZLE STICK

❸ METHOD

This Barbadian classic is covertly tropical. It has the appearance of a simple G&T, but with coconut water instead of tonic. Fresh and sweet, this tastes deceptively alcohol-light.

Pour the gin and lime juice into a highball glass over crushed ice, top with coconut water, add a swizzle stick and lime slice, to garnish.

BIG CARDOMOMMA'S HOUSE

❶ INGREDIENTS

½ MANGO, FRESH AND RIPE
25 ML (1 OZ) PEACH SCHNAPPS
1 TABLESPOON LIME JUICE, FRESHLY SQUEEZED
15 ML (½ OZ) HOMEMADE CARDAMOM
SYRUP (SEE PAGE 34) • CHAMPAGNE, TO TOP

❷ EQUIPMENT

TUMBLER   BLENDER   STRAINER

❸ METHOD

Cardamom, the subtle, warming spice, matches well with this mango lassi-like drink, topped up with champagne.

Peel and chop the mango and blend with peach schnapps, lime juice, cardamom syrup and ice cubes. Strain into a tumbler over ice cubes, top with champagne and serve.

PINEAPPLE MOUNTAIN

Dark, aged rum deepens this otherwise sweet kick of a drink. Homemade ginger syrup gives a warm edge and lemon keeps it tart.

Ingredients
50 ml (2 oz) aged rum
50 ml (2 oz) fresh pineapple juice
1 tablespoon lemon juice, freshly squeezed
1 tablespoon Ginger Syrup (page 34)
dash of Angostura bitters
slice of pineapple, to garnish

Glass
tumbler

Equipment
shaker

Method
Shake the rum, fruit juices and ginger syrup with ice cubes and vigour, strain into a chilled tumbler filled with ice cubes. Add a dash of Angostura bitters and garnish with a slice of pineapple.

FROZEN GINGER MARGARITA

This classic margarita mix – laced with fiery-sweet ginger syrup, lime zest and Cointreau – is topped up with chilled champagne in the glass.

Ingredients
50 ml (2 oz) tequila
25 ml (1oz) Cointreau
25 ml (1 oz) Ginger Syrup (see page 34)
juice and zest of ½ lime
1 tablespoon lemon juice, freshly squeezed
1 tablespoon orange juice, freshly squeezed
chilled champagne, to top
slice of lime, to garnish

Glass
tumbler

Equipment
blender, plastic container

Method
Add tequila, Cointreau, ginger syrup, lime juice and zest and the lemon and orange juices into a blender with ice cubes. Place in a freezer for 2 hours, or until partially frozen. Stir and top with champagne. Garnish with a slice of lime to serve.

WATERMELON BLOODY MARY

A summery, balcony BBQ update on the bloody classic, swapping out the Mary's savoury elements – tomato juice, Worcestershire and Tabasco – for fresh watermelon, Angostura bitters and a splash of white wine. For a single drink, you'll need about 150 g (5 oz) of fresh watermelon.

❶ INGREDIENTS

50 ml (2 oz) vodka
splash of dry white wine
150 ml (5 oz) watermelon juice, freshly blended
25 ml (1 oz) lemon juice, freshly squeezed
handful of mint leaves
pinch of coarsely ground pepper
dash of Angostura bitters
slice of watermelon to garnish

❷ EQUIPMENT

HIGHBALL   BLENDER   SHAKER

❸ METHOD

Shake the vodka, wine, fruit juices, mint, pepper and Angostura bitters with ice and vigour. Strain into a highball over ice cubes. Garnish with a watermelon slice.

THERE WILL
BE BLOOD

The spiced, soupy classic, seven ways: from the iconic Bloody Mary recipe to all its variations, with the heat turned up via Tabasco, fresh chilli, horseradish or wasabi and black pepper infused vodka, with a wiener thrown in for good measure. Master the basic recipe and give it your own tweaks.

BLOODY MARY

❶ INGREDIENTS

50 ML (2 OZ) VODKA • SPLASH OF DRY WHITE WINE
DASH OF TABASCO • DASH OF WORCESTERSHIRE SAUCE
150 ML (5 OZ) TOMATO JUICE
25 ML (1 OZ) LEMON JUICE, FRESHLY SQUEEZED
PINCH OF CELERY SALT • PINCH OF CAYENNE PEPPER
CELERY STICK, TO GARNISH

❷ EQUIPMENT

HIGHBALL   SHAKER

The bloodiest of all the bloody drinks – never
has a cocktail recipe been so debated. Tabasco
or fresh chilli? Vodka or gin? And just how many
drops of Worcestershire sauce? Follow this
classic recipe, but feel free to give Mary your
own special treatment. She likes it spicy, FYI.

❸ METHOD

Shake the ingredients with ice and vigour.
Strain into a highball over ice cubes.
Garnish with a celery stick.

FIRE IN THE BLOOD

The strong one. Fire in the Blood is sharp, fiery and sour, with pepper infused vodka, soft dill notes and a vinegary Dijon kick.

❶ INGREDIENTS

½ TEASPOON DILL, CHOPPED
½ TEASPOON DIJON MUSTARD • 3 DASHES OF TABASCO
4 DASHES OF WORCESTERSHIRE SAUCE
50 ML (2 OZ) BLACK PEPPER INFUSED VODKA (PAGE 34)
100 ML (4 OZ) TOMATO JUICE • 1 TABLESPOON LEMON
JUICE, FRESHLY SQUEEZED • PINCH OF CELERY SALT
PINCH OF FRESHLY GROUND BLACK PEPPER

❷ EQUIPMENT

HIGHBALL   SHAKER   MUDDLER

❸ METHOD

Muddle the dill, mustard, Tabasco and Worcestershire sauce in a shaker, then add the vodka, tomato and lemon juices, and ice. Shake with vigour, strain into a highball glass filled with ice cubes and serve garnished with celery salt and pepper.

SANGRITA

❶ INGREDIENTS

50 ML (2 OZ) TEQUILA • SPLASH OF DRY SHERRY
1 TEASPOON CREAMED HORSERADISH
DASH OF WORCESTERSHIRE SAUCE
150 ML (5 OZ) CLAMATO JUICE
25 ML (1 OZ) LEMON JUICE, FRESHLY SQUEEZED
PINCH OF CELERY SALT • PINCH OF CAYENNE PEPPER
CELERY STICK OR SLICE OF LEMON TO GARNISH

❷ EQUIPMENT

HIGHBALL   SHAKER

The tequila version. Sangrita mix is a mainstay of authentic tequila bars, a clamato-based mix with creamed horseradish (or fresh if you can get it), dry sherry for depth and tequila for a sense of danger.

❸ METHOD

Shake the ingredients with ice and vigour. Strain into a highball over ice cubes. Garnish with a celery stick or lemon slice and serve.

WASABIAN

❶ INGREDIENTS

½ TEASPOON WASABI • PINCH OF CELERY SALT
1 TABLESPOON LIME JUICE, FRESHLY SQUEEZED
DASH OF LEMON JUICE • 50 ML (2 OZ) VODKA
1 TABLESPOON SAKE • 25 ML (1 OZ) TOMATO JUICE
1–2 DASHES OF ANGOSTURA BITTERS

❷ EQUIPMENT

HIGHBALL   SHAKER   BAR SPOON

The addition of this Japanese horseradish-like condiment – and sake – adds a subtle fire to this otherwise classic cocktail. On no account get drunk and try snorting wasabi up your nose for a dare. It never ends well.

❸ METHOD

Stir the wasabi, celery salt, lime and lemon juices in a shaker to form a paste. Add the vodka, sake and tomato juice and shake over ice. Strain into a highball filled with ice cubes. Float a drop or two of bitters on top.

EMERGENCY

Cocktail ingredients – mixers, fruits, garnishes – should be fresh whenever possible. But when it's 1 a.m., you have an impromptu guest or three, and the liquor store is closed, the home mixer will need to forget the rules and think creatively. Trawl your kitchen cupboards, reach up to the top shelf and dust off what could otherwise be a rather unique concoction.

ALL-NIGHT BREAKFAST

The star ingredient in this gin-based cocktail is the sour-sweetness of marmalade, adding a fizzing intensity to the drink. Try for rindless marmalade – it's easier to strain – but don't worry if you're all out. Add a triangle of toast as a side garnish so you can miss breakfast.

Ingredients
50 ml (2 oz) gin
1 tablespoon Cointreau
1 teaspoon orange marmalade, rindless
dash of lemon juice
lemon peel, to garnish
orange peel, to garnish

Glass
martini or coupe

Equipment
shaker

Method
Shake the gin, Cointreau, marmalade and lemon juice over ice cunes, and strain into a chilled martini glass or coupe. Garnish with lemon and orange peel and serve.

THE JAM

A classic flip in form, but with a sweet berry kick. You can use any stray, toast-crumb-free pot of jam, but using dark berries gives the opaque drink a pink-blue hue. Add more ginger syrup to taste if you prefer your drink on the sour side.

Ingredients
50 ml (2 oz) gin
1 tablespoon lime juice, freshly squeezed
1 teaspoon blackcurrant jam
dash of Ginger Syrup (page 34)
1 egg white

Glass
martini or coupe

Equipment
shaker

Method
Shake the gin, lime juice, jam, syrup and egg white with ice cubes and vigour. Strain into a chilled martini glass or coupe, and serve.

DILL PICKLE G & T

All the delicate flavours of the dill pickle, but none of the vinegary sourness. Cucumber and gin is a perfect combination, and the dill adds a sweet, slightly savoury edge. Swap the dill for fennel tops or celery leaves if you want, but never mess with the cucumber.

Ingredients
¼ cucumber, cut into fingertip-sized chunks
pinch of chopped dill
1 tablespoon lemon juice, freshly squeezed
50 ml (2 oz) gin
chilled tonic water, to top
cucumber spear, to garnish

Glass
highball

Equipment
muddler

Method
Gently muddle the cucumber chunks and dill with lemon juice and gin. Add ice cubes, top with chilled tonic water and garnish with a cucumber spear.

THE LONG SHOT

A classic martini made dirty – and slightly Germanic – with a drop or two of sauerkraut brine. It seems an impossible concoction in the cold light of day, but in the early hours it seems – almost magically – to become less of a long shot.

Ingredients
50 ml (2 oz) dry gin
1 teaspoon dry vermouth
1 teaspoon sauerkraut brine
½ teaspoon sauerkraut, to garnish

Glass
martini or coupe

Equipment
shaker or mixing glass
strainer
stirrer

Method
Shake or stir the gin, vermouth and brine with ice cubes, then strain into a martini glass or coupe. Garnish with a couple of strands of sauerkraut.

MINI BAR

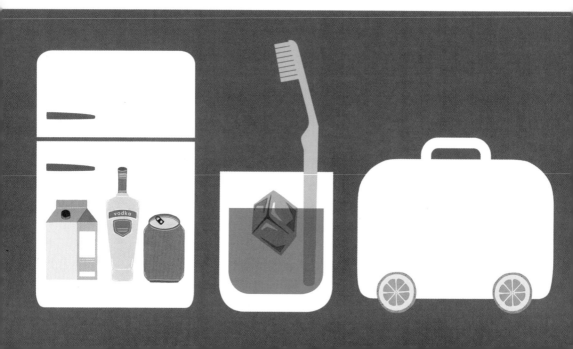

Holed up in a hotel with nothing but a credit card and a yearning to drink? Swing open the mini bar and use your mixologist skills for your own impromptu suite party. Chances are there'll be a corner store nearby: a squeeze of lemon, orange or lime; a bag of ice, and any sort of mixer can save a drink. But if not? Follow the recipes below. Just leave your dirty towels in the bath.

ROACH MOTEL

❶ INGREDIENTS

1 TEA BAG
1 TEASPOON BROWN SUGAR
50 ML (2 OZ) VODKA
165 ML (5½ OZ) BEER
LEMONADE, TO TOP

❷ EQUIPMENT

GLASS OR
TOOTHBRUSH BEAKER

KETTLE

CUP
OR MUG

A no-frills take on the beer tea punch,
lifting a pared-down mini bar selection
into something altogether magical.
And all too drinkable.

❸ METHOD

Make a cup of black tea with sugar, allow to
steep and cool, then remove the tea bag. Pour
the tea into a beaker, add vodka and beer, top
with lemonade and serve.

CALIMOCHO

❶ INGREDIENTS

125 ML (4½ OZ) RED WINE
125 ML (4½ OZ) COLA
SQUEEZE OF ORANGE JUICE (OPTIONAL)

❷ EQUIPMENT

GLASS OR
TOOTHBRUSH BEAKER

❸ METHOD

Add equal parts of wine and cola to a
toothbrush beaker and serve. Add ice cubes
and a squeeze of orange juice if available.

Aah, the Calimocho, the Latin-flavoured
drink that breaks all the rules: mixing red wine
with its diametric opposite, cola.
But, when drinking solely out of hotel
mini bars, needs must.

BATHTUB GIN

This drink should not be mixed in a bathtub, but drinking it perched on the edge of one – wearing nothing but a bath robe and a smile – is completely acceptable.

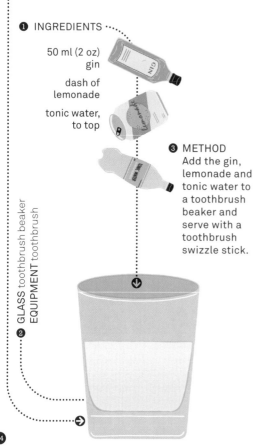

❶ INGREDIENTS

50 ml (2 oz) gin

dash of lemonade

tonic water, to top

❸ METHOD
Add the gin, lemonade and tonic water to a toothbrush beaker and serve with a toothbrush swizzle stick.

❷ GLASS toothbrush beaker
EQUIPMENT toothbrush

EARL GREAT MARTINI

Ice is essential for this one, the temperature will take the harshness off the spirits and lift the bergamot oil infused tea leaves to new heights. Otherwise it's just a couple of shots of booze with a tea bag thrown in. It's all in the eye of the beholder.

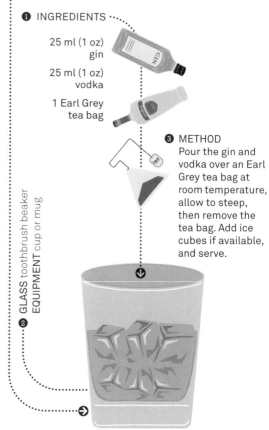

❶ INGREDIENTS

25 ml (1 oz) gin

25 ml (1 oz) vodka

1 Earl Grey tea bag

❸ METHOD
Pour the gin and vodka over an Earl Grey tea bag at room temperature, allow to steep, then remove the tea bag. Add ice cubes if available, and serve.

❷ GLASS toothbrush beaker
EQUIPMENT cup or mug

FOREAL BUCKS FIZZ

Imagine a Mimosa without all that annoying orange juice, but with a strong, orange-flavoured liqueur instead. Sound good? You've just made yourself a Foreal Bucks Fizz.

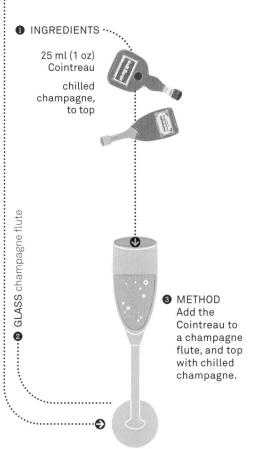

❶ INGREDIENTS

25 ml (1 oz) Cointreau

chilled champagne, to top

GLASS champagne flute

❸ METHOD
Add the Cointreau to a champagne flute, and top with chilled champagne.

DOOR SLAMMER

All that anonymity, those impossibly clean sheets: hotels are for doing almost anything in, you know, like in *Home Alone 2*. The Door Slammer is the drink that fuels the craziness, a slam-down orange and tequila shot with champagne bubbles to froth out your nose.

❶ INGREDIENTS

25 ml (1 oz) Cointreau

25 ml (1 oz) tequila gold

25 ml (1 oz) champagne

❸ METHOD
Add the Cointreau, tequila and champagne to a tough tumbler, cover with your hand, slam down on a hard surface and drink in one.

GLASS tumbler

THE **VIRGINS**

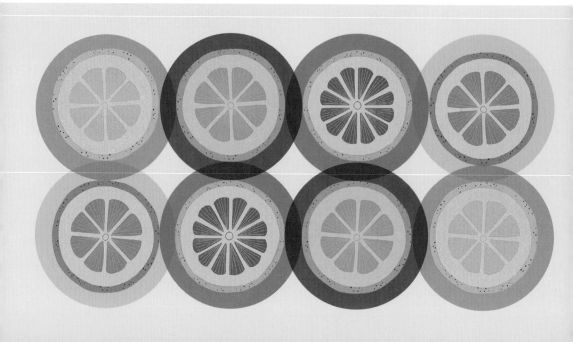

Why bother? That's what you're thinking, right? But it turns out some people don't drink – maybe they're driving, pregnant, or both at the same time. Or maybe they drank so much the night before they've awoken with their head on backwards? Either way, these people need help – and a good home mixer should see it as his duty to lend a hand. With great power, etc...

ST CLEMENTS

❶ INGREDIENTS

100 ML (3½ OZ) ORANGE JUICE,
FRESHLY SQUEEZED
100 ML (3½ OZ) BITTER LEMON
SLICE OF ORANGE, TO GARNISH
SLICE OF LEMON, TO GARNISH

❷ EQUIPMENT

HIGHBALL

A zingy little number and easy to mix.
The orange juice must be freshly squeezed,
with lots of fruit to garnish. Use blood oranges
to rosy things up.

❸ METHOD

Pour the orange juice and bitter lemon into
a highball filled with crushed ice, garnish
with orange and lemon slices and serve.

VIRGIN MARY

❶ INGREDIENTS

100 ML (3½ OZ) TOMATO JUICE • 2 DASHES OF TABASCO
4 DASHES OF WORCESTERSHIRE SAUCE • DASH OF LIME
JUICE, FRESHLY SQUEEZED • DASH OF LEMON JUICE,
FRESHLY SQUEEZED • PINCH OF CELERY SALT
PINCH OF FRESHLY GROUND BLACK PEPPER
1 CHERRY TOMATO, HALVED, TO GARNISH
1 CELERY STICK, TO GARNISH

❷ EQUIPMENT

HIGHBALL

SHAKER

❸ METHOD

For the embarrassed non-drinker, the perfect undercover alcohol-free drink. This is the classic recipe and best kept simple and fresh with lots of citrus to lend a little complexity.

Shake the tomato juice, Tabasco, Worcestershire sauce, lime and lemon juices over ice and strain into a highball with a ice cubes. Season to taste. Garnish with the tomato halves and celery stick and serve.

MINTED

The things you can do with a cucumber... This super-fresh cocktail is crying out for a shot of vodka, but is surprisingly tasty without.

Ingredients
½ cucumber, peeled
25 ml (1 oz) lime juice, freshly squeezed
dash of Mint Syrup (page 34), to taste
sparkling water, to top
small handful of mint leaves, to garnish

Glass
highball

Equipment
blender
fine gauge sieve

Method
Blend the cucumber with the lime juice, sieve and pour into a highball glass with a few ice cubes. Add the mint syrup, top with sparkling water, garnish with mint leaves and serve.

MANGO LASSI

The classic and bold, traditional Indian drink breaks the cardinal rule of mixing fruit, citrus, and dairy yoghurt, but somehow it works. Add more ice as you blend to create a lighter, less milkshake-like drink.

Ingredients
1 ripe mango, peeled, seeded and chopped
dash of lime juice, freshly squeezed
finely grated zest of ½ lime
500 ml (17 oz) natural yoghurt
dash of Cardamom Syrup (see page 34)

Glass
highball

Equipment
blender
strainer

Method
Blend the mango with the lime juice, zest, yoghurt, cardamom syrup and ice cubes. Strain into a highball filled with ice cubes and serve.

SODA BERRY

Ginger syrup is the key to this berry-packed concoction – it adds a sweet, fiery complexity to proceedings – and mint adds a bit of English countryside greenery: like eating a hedgerow.

Ingredients
4–5 blackberries
4–5 raspberries
handful of mint
dash of Ginger Syrup (page 34)
cream soda, to top
sprig of mint, to garnish

Glass
highball

Equipment
blender
bar spoon

Method
Blend the berries, mint leaves and ginger syrup with a handful of crushed ice, pour into a highball over ice cubes, top with cream soda, and stir. Garnish with a sprig of mint.

PIMMS STAND IN

A super-strong shot of black tea, and a dash of Angostura Bitters form the basis of this drink. A splash of tonic gives the impression of alcohol.

Ingredients
50 ml (2 oz) strong, chilled tea
50 ml (2 oz) tonic water
25 ml (1 oz) lime juice, freshly squeezed
chopped cucumber, to taste
3 strawberries
sprig of mint
lemonade to top
dash of Angostura Bitters

Glass
highball

Equipment
kettle and tea cup
knife and chopping board

Method
Make a cup of black tea, and chill it. Pour it into a shaker with lime juice and bitters, strain into a highball over ice cubes, fruit and mint. Add the tonic and top with lemonade.

SEASONAL

You wouldn't loaf about in the park in your Speedos in winter (right?), just like you wouldn't air out your thermal undies in the summer time. There's a time and a place, my friend – just like the seasonal cocktail. Cucumber Mint Gin Fizzes are for Spring, and Cardamom and Ginger Eggnog is really best enjoyed in the depths of Winter; thermal undies, notwithstanding.

SPRING:
BLUEBERRY HILLS

Fresh, plump blueberries, squished to within an inch of their former selves, dark rum, lime, mint and ginger ale. What's not to love? Don't skimp on the lime, it brings it all together.

❶ INGREDIENTS

7–10 blueberries, to muddle and garnish
sprig of mint
50 ml (2 oz) dark rum
25 ml (1oz) lime juice, freshly squeezed
ginger ale, to top

❷ EQUIPMENT

HIGHBALL   MUDDLER

❸ METHOD

Muddle 4–7 blueberries and the mint in a highball with a little crushed ice, add the rum and lime juice, more crushed ice and 3 whole blueberries, top with ginger ale and serve.

SPRING:
CUCUMBER MINT GIN FIZZ

You can do almost anything with a cucumber, but this is definitely in the top five. The secret is to infuse the gin for as long as possible and to serve the whole thing super-chilled.

❶ INGREDIENTS

1 cucumber, cut into spears
sprig of mint, bruised,
50 ml (2 oz) gin
dash of lemon juice, freshly squeezed
chilled tonic water, to top

❷ EQUIPMENT

HIGHBALL

WATER JUG

STRAINER

❸ METHOD

Add most of the cucumber spears and the mint to a jug, cover with the gin and chill for 2 hours in the fridge. Fill a highball with a few ice cubes, add a fresh cucumber spear and the lemon juice and strain the chilled, infused gin into the glass. Top with chilled tonic water.

SUMMER:
CHERRY MOJITO

Use really ripe, super-tender cherries for this one, they add a sweet flavour and bloody texture to proceedings and like all good Mojitos the flavours increase the more slowly you drink.

❶ INGREDIENTS

4–5 ripe fresh cherries, pitted
sprig of mint
1 teaspoon unrefined sugar
50 ml (2 oz) white rum
25 ml (1 oz) lime juice, freshly squeezed
sparkling water, to top

❷ EQUIPMENT

HIGHBALL   MUDDLER

❸ METHOD

Muddle the cherries, mint and sugar in a highball, with a little crushed ice, add the rum and lime juice, add more crushed ice and top with sparkling water.

SUMMER: PINK DOG

Vodka, tangy pink grapefruit, Campari and grenadine give this concoction a not-too subtle pink hue, like a bright lipstick.

❶ INGREDIENTS

sea salt flakes
50 ml (2 oz) vodka
25 ml (1 oz) pink grapefruit juice,
   freshly squeezed
25 ml (1 oz) Campari
dash of grenadine

❷ EQUIPMENT

MARTINI OR COUPE   SHAKER

❸ METHOD

Rim the glass with sea salt flakes, and chill. Shake the vodka, grapefruit juice, Campari and grenadine over ice cubes, strain into the prepared martini glass or coupe and serve.

AUTUMN: CRANBERRY ADAM

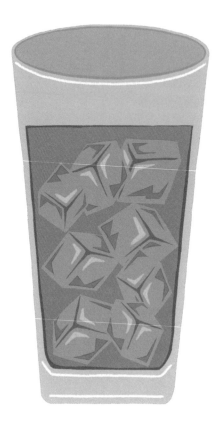

Ginger syrup and spiced rum (Sailor Jerry do a rather fine one) drags the Cranberry Adam from Cosmopolitan territory to something altogether more gruff and manly.

❶ INGREDIENTS

50 ml (2 oz) spiced rum
50 ml (2 oz) cranberry juice
dash of Ginger Syrup (page 34)
ginger beer, to top

❷ EQUIPMENT

HIGHBALL

❸ METHOD

Pour the rum, cranberry juice and ginger syrup into a highball filled with ice cubes, top with ginger beer and serve.

AUTUMN: CIDERHOUSE BLUES

A spicy, clove-scented cider packed with bourbon. Use good-quality cloudy apple juice and your own home-made clove syrup and don't skimp on the lemon juice.

❶ INGREDIENTS

50 ml (2 oz) bourbon
25 ml (1 oz) Clove Syrup (page 34)
dash of lemon juice, freshly squeezed
cloudy apple juice, to top
cinnamon stick, to garnish

❷ EQUIPMENT

HIGHBALL   SHAKER

❸ METHOD

Shake the bourbon, clove syrup and lemon juice over ice cubes, strain into a highball with 2–3 ice cubes, top with cloudy apple juice and garnish with a cinnamon stick.

WINTER:
MULLED POMEGRANATE WINE

Switching out orange juice for pomegranate is a smart move – it's the perfect basis for this rich mulled wine and the spiced rum and dash of Cointreau add the smell of pure festiveness, minus the turkey burps.

❶ INGREDIENTS

100 ml (4 oz) spiced rum
25 ml (1 oz) Cointreau
1.14 litres (38½ oz) pomegranate juice
1 bottle (750ml/25 oz) of red wine
2–3 whole cloves
dash of Ginger Syrup (see page 34)
3 cinnamon sticks
1 blood orange, sliced
fresh pomegranate seeds, to garnish

❷ EQUIPMENT

| HEATPROOF GLASS OR CUP | WOODEN SPOON | LARGE SAUCEPAN |

❸ METHOD

Add the ingredients (except the pomegranate seeds) to a large saucepan and heat gently for about 15 minutes, to allow the flavours to infuse. Stir occasionally with a wooden spoon. Serve in a heatproof glass or cup, adding the pomegranate seeds to garnish.

WINTER:
EGGNOG WITH CARDAMOM AND GINGER

THE holiday classic. Don't be scared of egg-based drinks, this one is ostensibly custard. With booze thrown in for good measure. And who doesn't want that? The cardamom pod (split open, but still whole) and ginger set it apart from the rest.

❶ INGREDIENTS

6 super-fresh organic eggs, beaten
1.14 litres (38½ oz) whole milk
50g (2 oz) unrefined sugar
3 cardamom pods, crushed
dash of Ginger Syrup (see page 34)
1 teaspoon cinnamon
200 ml (7 oz) brandy
pinch of freshly grated nutmeg, to garnish

❷ EQUIPMENT

HEATPROOF   WOODEN   LARGE
GLASS OR CUP   SPOON   SAUCEPAN   GRATER

❸ METHOD

Pour the beaten eggs into a saucepan with the milk, sugar, crushed cardamom pods, ginger syrup and cinnamon and heat gently, stirring occasionally, until the mixture thickens. Remove the cardamom pods. Share the brandy between individual heatproof glasses or cups, then pour over the warm eggnog (or chill first, if you like). Sprinkle with grated nutmeg and serve.

RETRO

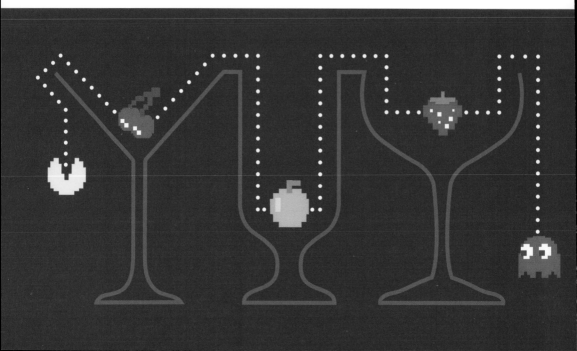

Remember the '80s? Mullet perms, big shoulders, chest hair – and that's just the women. Cocktail bars had neon signs and vest-wearing bartenders, and fruity drinks heaved under the weight of paper parasols and curly straws. Like other slightly embarrassing eras, there were some gems that are worth reliving.

TEQUILA SUNRISE

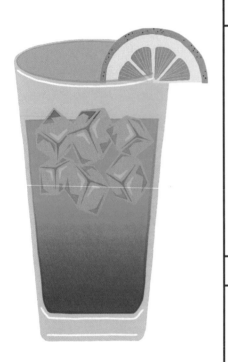

❶ INGREDIENTS

25 ML (1 OZ) TEQUILA
240 ML (8 OZ) ORANGE JUICE, FRESHLY SQUEEZED
DASH OF GRENADINE
ORANGE WEDGE, TO GARNISH

❷ EQUIPMENT

HIGHBALL

❸ METHOD

With its big flavours and wonderfully gimmicky two-tone, ombré styling, the Tequila Sunrise epitomises the '80s: cheap, garish, and kind of amazing.

Add ice cubes to a highball glass, up to the halfway mark. Add tequila, top with orange juice and – slowly – add the grenadine. Garnish with an orange wedge.

WHITE RUSSIAN

❶ INGREDIENTS

50 ML (2 OZ) VODKA
50 ML (2 OZ) SINGLE (LIGHT) CREAM
50 ML (2 OZ) KAHLUA

❷ EQUIPMENT

TUMBLER   SHAKER

❸ METHOD

As a rule, cocktails shouldn't be milky, but
this retro cocktail is one of the few exceptions.
The White Russian is delicious. And think of
all the calcium you'll be getting.

Shake the ingredients with ice cubes and
strain into a tumbler over ice cubes.

ZOMBIE

If any self-respecting zombie tried this drink they wouldn't even think about eating human brains or innards, they'd be taken away on a Caribbean fantasy, a dream of tropical beaches, sunsets, and lycra-clad lovelies.

❶ INGREDIENTS

25 ml (1 oz) light rum
25 ml (1 oz) golden rum
25 ml (1 oz) Jamaican rum
generous squeeze of lime juice
2 dashes of passion fruit juice
2 dashes of pineapple juice
dash of Simple Syrup (page 32), to taste
20 ml (¾ oz) overproof rum

❷ EQUIPMENT

HIGHBALL   SHAKER

❸ METHOD

Pour the light, golden and Jamaican rum into a shaker with the fruit juices and a dash of sugar syrup (to taste). Shake with ice and vigour, pour into a highball filled with ice, float the overproof rum on top.

BRANDY ALEXANDER

The Brandy Alexander makes the White Russian look like gone-off milk. The triple liquor mix is a rather classy addition, and the nutmeg garnish is brilliantly retro.

❶ INGREDIENTS

50 ml (2 oz) brandy
25 ml (1 oz) white crème de cacao
25 ml (1 oz) dark crème de cacao
1 tablespoon single (light) cream
pinch of freshly grated nutmeg, to garnish

❷ EQUIPMENT

MARTINI
OR COUPE

SHAKER

GRATER

❸ METHOD

Shake the brandy, crème de cacao and cream with ice cubes and vigour; strain into a chilled martini glass or coupe. Serve with a little freshly grated nutmeg on top.

AVIATION

This slightly creepy purple-hued classic looks sweet and unassuming, but it packs a punch: super-sour (even the maraschino liqueur does little to sweeten it) with a fragrant violet aroma.

❶ INGREDIENTS

50 ml (2 oz) gin
1 tablespoon lemon juice
2 teaspoons maraschino cherry liqueur
dash of crème de violette

❷ EQUIPMENT

MARTINI
OR COUPE

SHAKER

❸ METHOD

Shake the gin, lemon juice, cherry liqueur and crème de violette over ice cubes, and pour into a chilled martini glass or coupe.

BOULEVARDIER

This clever balance of sweet and sour – sweet vermouth and Campari – is kicked out of the park with a tough whisky hit. A retro bar classic.

❶ INGREDIENTS

25 ml (1 oz) whisky
25 ml (1 oz) Campari
25 ml (1 oz) sweet vermouth
orange peel, to garnish

❷ EQUIPMENT

TUMBLER   SHAKER

❸ METHOD

Shake the whisky, Campari, and sweet vermouth with ice then pour into a tumbler over a large cube of ice. Garnish with orange peel and serve.

GREYHOUND

50 ML (2 OZ) GIN
100 ML (3½ OZ) GRAPEFRUIT JUICE,
FRESHLY SQUEEZED
DASH OF AGAVE SYRUP

❷ EQUIPMENT

MARTINI OR COUPE   SHAKER

❸ METHOD

Shake the ingredients with ice cubes and vigour and pour into a chilled martini glass or coupe.

Refreshingly simple, a classic Greyhound only has two elements – gin and juice – but this version includes a little agave to take the edge off. Rosy it up with pink grapefruit juice instead of regular.

THE LAST WORD

❶ INGREDIENTS

25 ML (1 OZ) GIN
25 ML (1 OZ) LIME JUICE, FRESHLY SQUEEZED
25 ML (1 OZ) GREEN CHARTREUSE
25 ML (1 OZ) MARASCHINO CHERRY LIQUEUR

❷ EQUIPMENT

MARTINI OR COUPE   SHAKER

❸ METHOD

A dirty green cocktail, sour and sharp.
Like being slapped in the face by the Hulk.
And then tickled. And then slapped again.

Shake the ingredients with ice cubes and
vigour and pour into a chilled martini
glass or coupe.

DAN JONES

Perhaps the world's most prolific cocktail enjoyer, Dan Jones is a writer and editor living in London, having worked at a string of titles – from *i-D* magazine to *Time Out*. A self-professed homebody, he is well versed in the art of at-home drinking and loves to entertain, constantly 'researching' his cocktail craft and trying out new recipes. His favourite drink is a Dirty Martini. A really dirty one.

ACKNOWLEDGEMENTS

Thanks to Kate Pollard, Kajal Mistry and all at Hardie Grant UK; star designer Jim Green and amazing illustrator Esme Lonsdale; Gabriella Gershenson for introducing me to Sexy Baileys one New Year's Eve in NYC (a top-secret recipe); Tom McDonald for the constant supply of Aperol Spritz; Issy, Toby, and Arnold for taste-testing the Upcott, and my late, great grandparents for my first ever snifter of Cherry Brandy.

INDEX

The Mixers Manual by Dan Jones

First published in 2014 by Hardie Grant Books, an imprint of Hardie Grant Publishing

Hardie Grant Books (UK)
5th & 6th Floor
52–54 Southwark Street
London, SE1 1UN

Hardie Grant Books (Australia)
Ground Floor, Building 1
658 Church Street
Melbourne, VIC 3121

hardiegrantbooks.co.uk

British Library Cataloguing-in-Publication Data.
A catalogue record for this book is available from the British Library.

ISBN 978-174270-774-7

Publisher: Kate Pollard
Senior Editor: Kajal Mistry
Cover and Internal Design: Jim Green
Illustrator: © Esme Lonsdale
Editors: Zelda Turner and Lucy Bannell
Indexer: Cathy Heath
Colour Reproduction by p2d

Printed and bound in China by 1010